ST ANNES
THROUGH TIME
Peter Byrom

AMBERLEY PUBLISHING

I would like to dedicate this book to my wife and family for their patience and understanding over the past few years while I compiled it, especially Megan Sky Procter, my great granddaughter who knew nothing about it, being born on 10 January 2011. Also David, my son-in-law, for all his invaluable IT and technical assistance, and all the people who, in their various ways, helped me, whether they realise it or not.

First published 2012

Amberley Publishing
The Hill, Stroud
Gloucestershire, GL5 4EP

www.amberley-books.com

Copyright © Peter Byrom, 2012

The right of Peter Byrom to be identified as the
Author of this work has been asserted in accordance
with the Copyrights, Designs and Patents Act 1988.

ISBN 978 1 4456 0893 8

British Library Cataloguing in Publication Data.
A catalogue record for this book is available from
the British Library.

Typeset in 9.5pt on 12pt Celeste.
Typesetting by Amberley Publishing.
Printed in the UK.

Introduction

Since life, in whatever form, started to exist on this planet the importance of water for its survival has always been paramount; humans would eventually come to realise that it may also contain therapeutic qualities. The Romans developed bath houses in places such as Bath and Buxton, etc., for this purpose. In the eighteenth and early nineteenth centuries this was still believed; the wealthy would travel long distances to the Spa towns to partake in the mineralised waters by drinking or bathing in it.

Around this time it also became a popular belief that the sea waters around our coasts offered the same powers, and again this was only available to the locals or those who could afford to travel down long country lanes by coach and horses. The main area in Lancashire for this was the Fylde coast, namely Lytham and Blackpool. (My own namesakes, affluent business men from Manchester, one of the sons being John Byrom the poet, shorthand inventor and Jacobite supporter, travelled to the area to bathe in the sea and ride horses on the sands.)

The railway arrived in 1863, passing through Lytham to Blackpool from Preston carving its way through the sand dunes and rabbit warrens. This opened the coast to the masses from the mill towns of central Lancashire and further afield. As more people started to descend on the area, Elijah Hargreaves, in 1874, had a vision and leased 600 acres of these barren sand dunes from the Clifton Estate with a view to creating a new resort on the coast between Lytham and Blackpool, the area was known as Heyhouses on Sea. He formed the St Annes Land & Building Company, named after the Parish Church of St Anne that had been built by Lady Eleanor Cecil Clifton in 1873 and named after her mother. It was originally a Chapel of Ease attached to St Cuthberts Church in Lytham and built for the workers of the Heyhouses Hamlet, which was part of the Clifton Estate.

Elijah and the St Annes Land & Building Company's plans took a big leap forward in February 1875 when the first sod was cut. This was followed in March by the laying of the foundation stone by seven-year-old John Talbot Clifton (who later became Squire Clifton) of the first significant building in what was to become St Annes on the Sea, the St Annes Hotel, built near the railway station, a sign that they had their eyes on the tourist industry.

In the 1970s, St Annes still maintained a lot of its character and charm but moves were afoot, at great expense, to do a spot of modernisation and redevelopment, hopefully conserving and protecting what made it unique. In a way this book is about that journey.

Our journey mainly starts around the pier, then up the North Promenade, back to the pier and down St Annes Road West over the Crescent into St Annes Road East, eventually coming back and into Ashton Gardens before our journey along the South Promenade.

P. Byrom
2012

Rabbit Infested Sand Dunes

Trams travelling through the rabbit infested sand dunes from Gynn Square Blackpool to Lytham via St Annes. On the left is the Lemon Tree Housing complex (which used to be a casino) followed by Pontins Holiday Camp which closed down in 2009 and is currently being demolished.

St Annes Pier

The Pier, which opened in 1885, was originally 315 yards long with a 40-foot jetty to the shipping channel at the end. This was used by various styles of craft, especially pleasure boats which plied their trade from Liverpool to Morecambe calling at all ports on the way, including St Annes. The shipping channel silted up after the canalling of the River Ribble directly out to the open sea during the Second World War.

St Annes-on-Sea, The Pier.

The Moorish Concert Pavilion

The Moorish Concert Pavilion can be seen at the far end on the right. The new pier head with its mock-Tudor embellishments and handsome boardroom, kiosks and bandstand, etc., were added when the whole pier was widened at a cost of £30,000 in 1904. The Floral Hall at the end on the left was opened in June 1910. The pier was the main centre of entertainment until new distractions came along.

The Majestic Hotel I

The postcard picture was taken from the Majestic Hotel now demolished. The photograph below was taken from the block of apartments called the Majestic that replaced it.

NORTH PROMENADE. ST. ANNES-ON-THE-SEA.

North Promenade

The large sand dune at the back of the garden was removed to make room for a car park. After the statue of Les Dawson was erected in 2008, the garden was named 'The Peace and Sensory Garden'.

1545. SOUTHDOWN HOTEL FROM GARDENS, ST ANNES-ON-S

The Town Hall

The first building on the left was originally known as the Southdown Hotel, it is now the Town Hall.

SANDS & NORTH PROMENADE. ST-ANNES-ON-SEA.

Porritt Houses I

The North Promenade from the pier showing the Porritt houses. These were built in the 1890s using East Lancashire (Helmshore) stone and yellow brick.

The
Princes
Hotel

NORTH
PROMENADE
ST. ANNES-ON-SEA

Telephone :
St. Annes 25161-2
Private Exchange

The Princes Hotel

The Princes Hotel on the North Promenade was advertised as being 200 yards from the Pier and 5 minutes from the railway station and if customers used the entrance onto Clifton Drive they would be only 15 minutes from the nearest golf course.

Porritt Houses II

A lot of the properties along the North and South Promenades were constructed by a builder called Porritt and because of their distinctive style were affectionately known as 'Porritt Houses'. Apart from the Town Hall most of them on the South Promenade have either been demolished or incorporated into the present day hotels.

Ormerod Convalescent Home I

Ormerod Convalescent Home situated at the northern end of the North Promenade dates from 1890 and was named after Abraham Ormerod and used for the benefit of deprived children from the industrial towns of Lancashire. It was run by an Anglican Order of nuns, the Community of the Sisters of the Church based in Richmond Surrey. In 1970 MENCAP leased it and it was used as a home for the mentally handicapped.

SAS.146F ORMEROD HOUSE, ST. ANNES ON THE SEA

Ormerod Convalescent Home II

A side view of the Ormerod Home. Due to maintenance costs it was sold in 1984 and demolished to make way for a housing development. Before the demolition of the home, a beautiful Victorian mosaic depicting the nativity was removed from the chapel by the contractors who presented it to the nuns, who in turn gave it to St Margaret's Parish Church in St Annes for safekeeping.

THE BLACKBURN CONVALESCENT HOME ST ANNES

The Blackburn and District Convalescent Home

The Blackburn and District Convalescent Home was built in the sand dunes between St Annes and Blackpool in 1914. By 2005 it was a derelict property plagued regularly by vandals and set on fire. Its future looked bleak and many a proposal had been put forward on what to do with this blot on the landscape; in 2005 a development was started to convert it into apartments.

Pier Entrance and Southdown Hydro, St. Anne's-on-the-Sea   2601-9

The Pier Head
Pier Head entrance from the pier. Part of the five-paned, oblong window can just be seen in the blue band across the top of the photograph. The Southdown Hydro Hotel is on the left.

St Annes-on-Sea, Hotel Majestic.

North Side of the Pier
These views look inland from the north side of the pier towards the Majestic Hotel.

South Side of the Pier
These two views look inland from the south side of the pier at the Town Hall and the start of the South Promenade.

The New Pavilion, St. Anne's-on-the-Sea

Floral Hall and Moorish Pavilion

The two main places of entertainment on the pier were the Floral Hall, opened in 1910 (known by the locals as the Tyrolean), and the Moorish Pavilion. The Moorish Pavilion was destroyed by fire in July 1974 and the Floral Hall suffered the same fate in 1982 and what was left of that end of the pier was later demolished.

Remains of the Pier
The remains of the end of the pier after it was demolished by fire.

The Majestic Hotel II

Imperial Hydro later became known as the Majestic Hotel. The main entrance was originally in the middle on the front, but due to bad weather and the amount of sand that blew across the road from the sand hills it was seldom used; a side entrance was used instead. The statue on the roof in the middle is, some say, Boadicea while others say Hygeia. The hotel was demolished in 1975 to make way for the Majestic Apartments.

Majestic Hotel III

The statue on the roof holding a trident and seen driving a team of horses was removed during the Second World War and melted down as part of St Annes contribution to the war effort. A friend of the compiler told him that when he was a teenager in the 1930s his friend managed to gain access to the roof and hung a chamber pot from the trident on the statue out of devilment and was severely reprimanded.

THE CHILDREN'S POOL, ST. ANNES-ON-THE-SEA.

Southdown Hydro

Looking past the boating pool and bandstand, on the right is the Southdown Hydro which was run by Miss Spyree who described it as being in 'the best situation facing pier and sea'.

St Annes Road West I
St Annes Road West was originally called Middle Lane and was wedged on either side by vast expanses of rabbit warren infested sand hills stretching from Squires Gate to Ansdell.

St. Annes Road West

St Annes Road West II
St Annes Road West is seen here from the pier head entrance. The open area on the left was where the Imperial Hydro (Majestic Hotel) was to be built.

St. Annes-on-the-Sea.
St. Annes Road, West.

St Annes Road West III

St Annes Road West looking inland from the junction with Clifton Drive towards the railway station between the trees in the distance. On the left behind the tall shrubbery are equally high imposing buildings, similar to the ones on the right, with enclosed, railed front gardens which were eventually removed when the houses were converted into shops making the Square the main shopping area of the town.

The Square I
The Square looking west.

The Square II
The Square looking east.

Crescent Bridge

This picture was taken from very close to where the original pedestrian crossing over the railway line was before the Crescent Bridge was built. In the postcard note the man with the brush is heading off to clean up a pile of horse manure in the street.

The Square III
St Annes Square from the Crescent Gardens with the pier head in the distance.

The Crescent

This photograph was taken looking eastwards up the Crescent from the town centre in early 1900s. Horse and carts, horse-drawn taxis, bicycles and pedestrians had the road to themselves.

A Closer View of the Crescent

In this area stood cowsheds, stables and whitewashed cottages. The road to the left of the trees was the original road over the railway track. On the opposite side of the tracks to the left, down a back alley, can be found a large building which used to be the stables for Whitesides horse-drawn taxis, it is now used as a bed centre.

The Crescent Gardens

The sepia photograph depicts a woman in a fine hat reading in Crescent Gardens. The photograph below is a view of the same spot today.

ST. ANNES ON SEA. DRIVE AND ELECTRIC CARS.

Public Transport

In this photograph trams and buses are seen at the junction of Clifton Drive and St Annes Road West. The two small hexagonal buildings on the left at the front of the bottom picture were originally tram waiting rooms. They eventually became the Tourist Information Office. They were closed in 2010 due to financial savings by the council and were later opened as a café.

Top of the Crescent, *c.* 1880, Looking East

The St Annes Chapel of Ease can be seen in the distance, built for the farmers and fishermen in the Heyhouses district, an area that was yet to be developed. The Mother Church was St Cuthberts Parish Church at Lytham. The houses on the right in the postcard are in what is now St Davids Road South and have been converted into shops.

Beauclerk Gardens

Beauclerk Gardens on St Annes Road East were donated by the Cliftons so that families would have an area to play and relax. Opened in 1924 they covered an area of 4,265 square yards. During alterations in 1961 while removing some old tree roots, an earthenware pot, containing 383 coins and dating between 1550 and 1644, was found by workman Douglas Jeffrey; it became known as the St Annes hoard.

ST. ANNES HOTEL , ST.-ANNES-ON-SEA.

St Annes Hotel

St Annes started with the building of the St Annes Hotel in 1875 and it opened in 1876. The hotel also acted as the headquarters of a golf club whose first tee was close to the railway station. There was also a bowling green and stables at the hotel – the perfect start of a town for tourists. Demolished in 1985 it is now known as the Town House.

Wood Street

Note all the houses with their walled, shrub and tree filled front gardens, all removed for parking when the houses were converted into shops. At the top end on St Annes Road South stand two shops looking down Wood Street; the one on the left was the town's first post office called Alpha House. A sandstone block found during renovation was inscribed: 'ALPHA 1875 HOUSE' and is now inserted under the window.

Clifton Drive South

Trams travelling north along Clifton Drive South from Lytham, heading for St Annes Square then on to Squires Gate and Gynn Square, Blackpool.

'Richard Peck House', RAF Convalescent Home
The postcard is signed on the back by many of the residents who once lived there.

Kilgrimol School, St.-Annes-on-the-Sea

Kilgrimol School

Kilgrimol School was founded by John Allen in 1875 aided by his wife. In 1892 he went into partnership with Mr J. F. Davenport and a few years later after the loss of his wife he retired and opened a herbalist shop in Park Road. He committed suicide in 1904. Mr and Mrs Davenport developed the school to a high standard before retiring in 1913; Mr Davenport died in 1915 aged sixty-three.

Seabright
'Seabright' convalescent home is now the Clifton Academy.

Ashton Gardens I

The entrance to Ashton Gardens from Clifton Drive North. The gateway area was used as a builders' yard by Porritt when he was building the houses on the promenade.

WAR MEMORIAL, ST ANNES-ON-SEA.

War Memorial

The War Memorial was a gift from the Rt. Hon. Lord Ashton. The female figure on the top typifies the birth of a new life after the hardships of fierce warfare. It was unveiled on Sunday 12 October 1924.

Ashton Gardens II
Ashton Gardens entrance on Clifton Drive North from the War Memorial.

Ashton Gardens III
Ashton Gardens with Beach Road at the back.

Ashton Gardens IV

A view of stepping stones over the water leading to the lake from a wooded area – most of the stones were removed during the twentieth century and dumped on the bank for 'Health and Safety' reasons.

Ashton Gardens V
Ashton Gardens and the fountain in the background.

Ashton Gardens VI
A view of the kiosk beside the lake.

THE BRIDGE,
ASHTON GARDENS,
ST. ANNES-ON-SEA.

Ashton Gardens VII
Ashton Gardens ornamental bridge.

ASHTON GARDENS, ST. ANNES-ON-SEA.

Ashton Gardens VIII
Flower garden viewed from the ornamental bridge.

Rose Gardens, Ashton Park, St. Annes-on-Sea

Ashton Gardens IX

These two photographs show the rose garden. After some years had passed the statue in the pond in the middle was removed for safe keeping – so safe, apparently, that no one knows where it is.

Ashton Gardens X
More views of the rose garden.

54

THE ROSE GARDEN, ASHTON GARDENS, LYTHAM ST. ANNES

Ashton Gardens XI
Rose garden drinking fountain.

Ashton Gardens XII
Tennis courts backing onto St Georges Road.

Tennis Courts, Ashton Gardens, St. Annes-on-the-Sea.

Ashton Institute

The Ashton Institute was removed with the promise to rebuild it (saving as much as possible) near the gardens entrance in St Georges Road. The land it was on was wanted, along with the Plaza Bingo and car showroom sites in St Georges Road, to build the apartments known as Ashton View. Due to damp and wood worm very little of it was saved.

Ashton Pavilion

Ashton Pavilion at St George's entrance burnt down in 1977. After many years of plans and discussions and no agreements they ran out of money so nothing was done until the massive refurbishment of 2010–12. The Ashton Institute was rebuilt on the site of the original Pavilion.

Empire de Lux Picture House

Empire de Lux Picture House in St Georges Road opened in 1912 as a single-storey building with a large pitched roof and arched façade. The roof was removed and another floor added accessed by the stairs on the left hand side. It later became the Plaza Bingo Hall with a casino above.

THE BEACH, FROM THE PIER,
ST. ANNES-ON-SEA.

Beach and Promenade

The photograph above depicts much busier times on the beach and promenade than today. The building on the extreme left at the back is the St Ives Hotel which began life as a school. The white building just off centre with three 'crow stepped gables' on the front is the original Fernlea before it was vastly extended, and the building to the right of it has been developed into the Dalmeny hotel.

Sands and Pier from South Promenade
Both of these views show just how popular the beach has remained through time.

St Annes Beach

The postcard shows the beach, *c.* 1920, with a very busy pier. The hut near the water's edge has a large 'Mixed Bathing' notice on the roof.

THE PROMENADE AND ENTRANCE TO PIER, ST. ANNES-ON-SEA.   H.7335.

South Promenade

Views of the South Promenade and the entrance to the pier.

Promenade Gardens and Lifeboat Memorial, St Annes-on-Sea

South Promenade Gardens and Lifeboat Monument

Five days before the worst event in lifeboat history, which was to be the reason for the construction of this monument, the St Annes lifeboat crew saved six men from the *Yan Yean* near Salters Bank.

THE MONUMENT, ST. ANNES-ON-THE-SEA

Lifeboat Monument

The Lifeboat Monument was unveiled in May 1888 to commemorate the thirteen strong crew of the lifeboat *Laura Janet* from St Annes and the fourteen lifeboatmen of the *Eliza Fernlea* from Southport who lost their lives trying to save the crew of the barque *Mexico* which had gone aground in a storm in the River Ribble in December 1886. The loss of these men left sixteen widows and fifty orphans.

Collegiate School, St. Annes

The Collegiate School St Annes
The Collegiate School St Annes stood where the St Ives Hotel now stands. The outline can still be seen in the structure of the hotel with its apexes.

Esplanade Gardens

The Victorian Fountain in the Esplanade Gardens was laid out between 1907 and 1914.

South Promenade Gardens, Looking South

The flowers haven't quite bloomed in the modern photograph below. Note the ever-present traffic on the roads.

South Promenade Gardens, Looking North
In these two photographs the flowers are out for all to enjoy.

Seaward Side of Promenade Boating Lake
There are not many boats out in these two photographs.

Promenade Side of the Boating Lake

The sepia photograph above shows just how popular the boating lake was, particularly among children. The modern photograph depicts how things have irrevocably changed.

The Roman Style Open Air Baths
The building where the original picture was taken from has long since disappeared and private apartments have been built on the site. The area of the baths is now a built up entertainment complex with an indoor swimming pool, most of which was closed down in 2008/09, including the pool for financial reasons. The pool was reopened halfway through the 2010 holiday season.

The Roman Baths, Looking South
The domed towers of the Grand Hotel can be seen on the left.

Bathing Pool, St. Annes-on-Sea   11602

The Roman Baths

The access without barriers to the top of the slide at the open air baths would not pass any Health and Safety laws today, but was a popular feature of the bathers.

Miniature Railway

The South Promenade miniature railway has been a favourite attraction for young and old alike for many decades.

Amphitheatre

The Amphitheatre bandstand was removed when it was decided only one was needed on the Promenade. The remaining oval area was used for open-air shows before being converted into a children's paddling pool, which, being too costly to maintain, the council decided, according to the local paper of 25 August 2004, to fill it in and plant it up with shrubs. To date this has not happened.

Promenade, St. Annes-on-Sea

South Promenade I
Photographs of the South Promenade walk from Beach Café to the pier.

South Promenade Gardens

The South Promenade Gardens are in a bad state of repair.

South Promenade, St. Annes-on-Sea

South Promenade II

South Promenade looking north from Eastbank Road showing the amount of redevelopment or demolition of the properties built in the late 1800s on this side of the pier. The empty space on the right is where the Grove Rest Home stood prior to demolition in 2005; it was the last of the Porritt-style buildings on this side.

Dalmeny Hotel
Note the large amount of redevelopment that has taken place over the years.

Clifton Hotel
Clifton Hotel, 49 South Promenade, was demolished shortly after the Second World War ended to build the block of private apartments known as the De Vere Gardens.

Wesleyan Church and East Bank Road, St. Annes-on-the-Sea

Birling Bros., Publishers and Printers, St. Annes-on-the-Sea.

Drive Methodist Church

The back of the Drive Methodist Church was originally the Wesleyan Chapel built in 1892. The red-bricked, red-roofed building before it is the old lifeboat house which was in use from 1879 to 1925. It is now a funeral director's.

Grand Hotel
The Esplanade Gardens in front of the Grand Hotel were created in 1914.

PROMENADE, ST. ANNES-ON-SEA.

Esplanade Gardens I

Apart from the pier head and Town Hall in the distance, the Grand Hotel is the only remaining original building left from those shown on the postcard.

Alpine Gardens

The photographs depict Alpine Gardens walk along the top of the sand hills on the South Promenade.

THE WATERFALL
PROMENADE GARDENS, ST. ANNES·ON·THE·SEA
A 569

Esplanade Gardens II

A manmade waterfall and grotto situated in the Esplanade Gardens opposite the Grand Hotel. At the time of construction around 350 gallons of water was pumped over it per minute, a great deal more than today. It is a favourite place for newlyweds to be photographed.

The Bridge, New Promenade Gardens, St. Anne's-on-Sea.

Promenade Gardens and Rockery Bridge

The Gregson family designed and laid out the Promenade Gardens and Rockery Bridge. The bridge was completed in 1909 and it is reputed that a workman placed a time capsule under it during its construction.

STEPPING STONES, PROMENADE GARDENS, ST. ANNES-ON-THE-SE

Esplanade Gardens III
Two views of the stepping stones in Esplanade Gardens.

Chadwick Hotel
Chadwick Hotel is the last hotel on the South Promenade.

Parish Church, St. Annes-on-Sea

St Annes Parish Church I
The entrance to St Annes Parish Church has a short section of road where hearses and wedding limousines can draw up in front safely.

ENTRANCE TO PARISH CHURCH, ST. ANNES-ON-THE-SEA.

St Annes Parish Church II
The church lychgates were at one time situated on the corner of Church Road and St Annes Road East. The church originally had a spire on the roof.

St Annes Parish Church III
The postcard shows the church with its new tower added in 1900.

St Annes Parish Church IV

St Annes Parish Church seen from the lychgate on the corner of St Annes Road East and Headroomgate Road. The church seats around 400 parishioners and has a peal of bells donated by Lady Eleanor Clifton. A peal of bells consists of eight bells, one for each note of the musical scale.

St. Thomas Church, St. Anne's-on-Sea

93727

St Thomas Church on Central Drive South

The notice under the street name sign on the postcard reads 'Chars a Bancs Prohibited'. Apparently these signs appeared on many street corners earning St Annes the name of the 'Forbidden City'.

Congregational Church, St. Annes-on-the-Sea

Congregational Church

Congregational Church, St Annes, was founded in 1885 and joined forces with the English Presbyterian Church to become the United Reformed Church. There is no graveyard.

Lytham and St Annes Golf Club

Lytham and St Annes Golf Club became the Royal Lytham St Annes Golf Club in 1926. The Club House was opened in 1898. The extension on the left hand side was constructed for the President's Office.